Julia Mewes has always had an unsurpassed passion for all animals. Growing up in a household without pets, she would do anything to get closer to any creatures, big or small - from mucking out stables for the chance to ride a horse, to saving a poorly bat in the school toilet.

Julia confirmed her calling when she visited a veterinary practice for the first time at the age of 15. This motivated her to aim for vet school and she successfully secured a place at Cambridge University in 1983. During her studies, she found joy in visiting stables, kennels and all different types of veterinary practices. She made sure to stay close to the animals by seeking lots of practical experience (and riding the horses at the end of the day, of course).

Once graduated in 1989, she continued to live her dream through the seven years she spent as an employed Veterinary Surgeon. When she had ideas for improving the practice, she took the leap of faith to start her own Clinic, which celebrated its 20th anniversary in June 2016.

Today, her unconditional love for animals remains unchanged. She sincerely wishes that this book will give you as much joy as animals give her, whilst helping to make sure your cat lives a long and healthy life.

CONTENTS

Caring for your Older Cat

CHAPTER 1
BEST CARE POSSIBLE

Your new pet deserves the best care possible, and we're here to help you make the right choices every step of the way

Congratulations on offering a loving home to your new friend. It is an exciting moment, and I present this book to you in the hope that it will help you enjoy your pet for a 'purringly' long time.

You want the very best for your new pet, but on the occasions when you are not sure which way to turn, this book is designed to inform you and support you in your choices. It is set out in two parts: things you might like to think about now, at the start of your relationship with a new furry friend, and then how to look out for and manage some of the common issues that may arise as he or she gets older.

I have been passionate about caring for pets since I was young, and have devoted my life to them. I worked as hard as I could in school to get the highest possible grades so that I could fulfil my dream - getting into Cambridge University's Vet School in 1983.

I qualified in 1989, and have now been a Vet for over 25 years. I even won a Lifetime Achievement Award in the JSPC Business Matters Awards 2014 in recognition of this devotion.

I have selected and trained my own team of experienced, compassionate professionals to ensure that all the pets we treat are given the very best care. My team are so well thought of by our clients that we were presented with a Customer Service Award the first time we entered a competition in the JSPC Business Matters Awards 2014, a local competition for all types and sizes of business in Mid Sussex, arranged by the team at the Mid Sussex Times.

Thanks to modern feeding methods and standards of veterinary care, I now expect most cats to live happily for 16 to 20 years. This little book may help to ensure that your new pet can also have a long, happy, healthy life.

I am not going to try to mention every possible disease or problem that your cat may experience, so if you cannot find the information you need in here, please visit the Symptom Checker on my website at:
www.themewesvets.co.uk/symptom-checker
or phone my caring and friendly team on 01444 456886.

CHAPTER 2
INTRODUCING YOUR CAT

Giving your kitty the time and space they need to settle in will make sure they're happy in their new home

Bringing home a new cat is an exciting time, but remember how nerve-wracking this might be for your new friend. However caring and genuine your intentions are, it's all a new experience for your little cat.

Julia's Mewesings:

My two new patients, Terry and June, were very lucky. A delightful black and white brother and sister, they had never been separated, so the rescue society was especially pleased to find a home for them together...until they heard that their new owner was planning to bring Terry back to them.

"He keeps peeing on my bed!" his new owner complained.

"I wash the sheets but he does it again the next day - it's disgusting!"

Luckily, the problem was soon resolved. After a careful health check and a urine sample I was able to reassure Terry's owner that he was not experiencing an infection or other bladder irritation, he was just upset by moving home.

We offered advice and support, combined with soothing pheromone treatment, and he gradually became the perfect clean feline companion they had hoped for.

One of the fun things about being a cat owner, however, is how different their little characters can be. Some will adapt to new surroundings really quickly, whereas others may take weeks to even start to want a cuddle.

My advice to you would be to allow them to set the pace. Many cats will spend the first few days hiding under the first piece of furniture they see, only coming out when all is quiet. You should allow this, and not force your attention onto them yet. Encourage your children to do the same.

It is usual to keep any cat in a new home indoors for the first three weeks.

This allows them to get to know their new home and start feeling secure there before they venture out into the wider world.

Make sure you provide a litter tray for them, and a scratch post if possible. If you have rooms where you would prefer to protect the carpet and door posts, these might be best kept out of bounds until your little one has started going outside!

Most cats coming from a rescue environment will already be litter trained - cats are fastidiously clean - but like Terry, they may urine mark if upset by the trauma of moving home.

Urine marking is different to 'having an accident'. Cats use urine marking to mark their new territory, and to express themselves when they are feeling a little out of their depth. It is thought that the smell of their own urine on vertical objects, or mixed with your smell, helps them to feel more confident. However, they might choose to do this on your laundry pile, or in your bed, which is not the nicest for you!

Try to be patient. It is usually a phase that passes as they settle in. Never punish your pet if he or she does this, as punishment will make them feel even more distressed.

There are lots of positive things you can do to help them get past this phase. If you need support on this, feel free to call the friendly team at The Mewes Vets on 01444 456886 for help.

If you already have other pets, you will know that it is not reasonable to expect them to be best friends immediately. You should start by allowing them to see, hear and smell each other, but not actually touch straight away.

A good way to do this is to keep them in separate areas of the house most of the time. When you are yourself feeling relaxed and calm, place the new pet inside a large, secure box which you can place on the edge of your settled pet's favourite areas. Allow them to interact through the bars every day until you feel sure that no fighting will occur, but don't keep them locked up for too long, as exercise and exploring are important too.

To read more about introducing new pets to settled pets or to babies go to www.newpetsinthehome.co.uk

Key Points from this chapter:

- **Be gentle and understanding when your cat arrives in its new home for life. They may take a few weeks to settle down.**

- **Never punish them if they have an accident - ask for professional support.**

CHAPTER 3
WEIGHT ISSUES

Being overweight is as much of a problem for your cat as it would be for you, so make sure you keep an eye on their waistline

Your pet is an individual. That's what makes having a cat such fun - their temperaments. Some are loving and cuddly, others distant and demanding. And many have very distinct ideas about what they are and are not prepared to eat!

The good news is that most pets that have been rehomed from a cattery will have had to learn that when it comes to food, the general rule is 'eat now or do without'. You may find it helpful to continue this regimen, at least at first. Despite what you sometimes read, not all cats seem to know the type and amount of food that is really healthy for them.

Julia's Mewesings:

Sylvester was truly enormous when he was rescued. I went to lift him up in his box, and needed an assistant to help get him off the ground!

He had lived with an ailing elderly person who truly loved him. Her love had gradually evolved into an unnatural feeding habit, without much exercise, and he had grown and grown. He had reached a stage where he barely moved, and when he did walk his stomach nearly touched the ground.

He came to us when his new owner acquired him, and he tipped the scales at 8.8kg - nearly double the size he should have been.

We counselled his new owner about the risks Sylvester faced in his future as an immensely obese animal: joint disease, heart disease, liver disease and diabetes to name a few. Luckily she was very open to giving him the healthiest possible future and immediately signed him up for Animal Weight Watchers.

With an appropriate low calorie diet we were able to retrain his stomach without hunger pangs, and luckily he adored chasing a feather on a string, so games became a regular part of his daily routine. The more he played the slimmer he became, and he is now a significantly more healthy 6.2kg, and much more muscular, going out and socialising in the village.

To keep your pet happy and healthy well into old age, talk to your vet about the optimal weight for your specific companion. Some cats have special nutritional requirements, and your vet will advise you about this as your cat's health evolves over time.

It is also fascinating for me to note in the consulting room that those cats that hunt and eat wildlife have the very best dental health. Those who eat an exclusively dry complete biscuit food have the next best teeth, but those on a high proportion of pouched or tinned wet foods have consistently worse teeth, and often lose them prematurely.

So when considering which food to choose, ask your vet for a recommendation, bearing in mind your cat's current medical health and dental status. I always select the healthiest choice for a long, happy, healthy life, at the best possible price for you too.

For my top five tips on how to help your overweight cat become more active, visit: www.fightingthepetflab.co.uk

Key Points from this chapter:

- **A good quality diet really does make all the difference to the health of your pet.**

- **Biscuit foods are generally better for dental health than tins or trays of food.**

- **Being overweight is a real threat to your cat's long term health and happiness.**

CHAPTER 4
WHAT'S NORMAL

Knowing what's normal for your pet is essential when it comes to their health care

Julia's Mewesings:

Jasmine arrived at the Clinic in her usual way: loudly complaining. With massive feline threats emitting from her cat carrier, I knew at once that I was in trouble.

Usually her complaints stop once her carrier opens on the consulting table, but this time she continued her chorus - letting me know in no uncertain terms that on this occasion she was really in need of my help.

It took a while to calm her, but eventually she allowed me to look into her bloodied ear and make some sense of her symptoms. She had a one-sided ear canal infection with an unpleasant smelly discharge, and the pain was putting her off her food and driving her distracted.

I decided to arrange a two-phase cure. First I would manage the pain and reduce the infection using long acting injections. Three days later I could see her again, maybe sedate her a little and with the swelling having reduced, irrigate her ear, find out how the problem started, and start ear drops to really get rid of the problem.

If only animals could talk! I imagine it must have taken days for Jasmine's ear to reach that extreme of discomfort, but being a feline of character, she wouldn't dream of complaining, so her owner was completely unaware of the problem until poor Jasmine couldn't bear it any longer.

Learn how to spot if your cat has an ear infection by downloading our free guide.
Visit: www.preventingfelineearinfections.co.uk

Whenever I give a talk at a school or nursery, I focus on these points:

- Pets are unable to speak to us in English and tell us when they have a dull ache, or a subtle pain.

- Animals tend to deliberately conceal pain until it is unbearable, in case the weakness puts them at risk from predators.

- Knowing what is normal behaviour for your pet is the only way you can then recognise when they are not behaving normally, and have a clue that they need to be taken to the vet.

It is so obvious, but sometimes it is helpful to think about the obvious. If your pet is normally up for a game of ball chasing, or usually greets you with a lovely ankle rub every morning, and then one day they are curled up in a ball and ignore you - there must be something wrong.

If they normally are begging for food at exactly the same time of day, every day, and immediately gorge the lot down in one go, then one day they just pick at it and wander off - something is wrong.

But how can you tell what the problem is?

Sometimes you can't, and that's when you have to make a decision whether to take them to the vet. Quite often a phone call with the sympathetic veterinary receptionist will help to clarify whether you have a problem, and if so, how urgent it is. All my receptionists are pet lovers and most are either qualified Registered Veterinary Nurses (RVNs), or in training to become RVNs. They are very highly trained, experienced and caring people, who really understand your concerns.

Even if your pet is behaving normally, you want them to stay as healthy as possible, so here is a little routine that may help you: Get into the habit of checking their eyes, ears, teeth, claws, skin and coat every day.

This takes only a few moments, and can become part of your cuddle routine each day. When stroking your pet, look carefully at their face, especially the eyes, for signs of unusual weeping or discharge. You will notice at once if one or both eyes are a bit winky or half closed. These would be reasons to see the vet.

Politely have a quick look in each ear, and a gentle sniff. An infection will often create an abnormal discharge, and a bit of a smell. Notice the normal colour of the skin in her ear, and the freckles. Then you will recognise if this changes and gets inflamed. Ideally, gently pop your index finger into the opening of the ear canal every day. That way, if ever you have to administer ear drops and massage them down, or if I have to use my auroscope to see into the ear, we won't be offending your feline friend unduly.

When your cat yawns, grab a quick look at their teeth, and occasionally a quick sniff. We are aiming to keep them lovely and white, with no reddening of the gums, and no foul smell. Again, if you can gently run your fingers over the back teeth on either side every day, you would be preparing your pet for later tooth brushing, as this becomes necessary.

Be aware that their claws do grow over time, and that some cats are quite inefficient with their clawing technique. So even if they will use the scratch post, aim to look at all the claws on their paws (five on the front - don't forget the little thumb or dew-claw - and four on the back, usually) at least once a week. You could check one paw every other day, for instance. If they are getting caught up in your carpet or clothing it may be time for a trim.

To see the claws, you can wait until your cat is padding your lap to take a sneaky peek, or when they are snoozing, respectfully pick up a paw and gently push up on the pad and down on the toes to cause the claws to extend for inspection.

And finally, as you enjoy some serious loving, running your hand or a brush over the lovely soft coat, have a quick look at the condition of the fur, and for signs that the skin is not happy - scurf, inflammation, spots or bleeding. We have a number of cranky cats at The Mewes Vets whose long coats have got out of control, and who have 'cattitude' about being brushed regularly by their owners. Our only option is to anaesthetise them in order to shave off all the matted fur that builds up over the months, and it makes me feel really sad that we have to do this, rather than manage them with grooming at home.

There are videos to show you how to do all of this at
www.themewesvets.co.uk/the-urban-vet

Performing these little tasks regularly will give you two advantages: you will get to know what is normal for your furry friend, and you are really likely to spot a problem evolving early on, which makes it easier for me and so cheaper for you to treat.

Use your eyes, finger tips, ears and nose - I always sniff a pet's ears & breath, and can often detect a problem before it is otherwise visible.

Julia's Mewesings:

I met a beautifully coiffed and manicured lady once who brought her obviously much loved Pandora to see me for a routine appointment. I was captivated by the sparkly nail varnish the owner had selected for a Christmas party, but less impressed with Pandora's manicure.

Unbelievably Pandora was walking around with no limp, despite three of her claws having grown into her own pads. She was effectively walking with large thorns being forced deeper into her own flesh with every stride. Why didn't she complain? Her loving owner would have brought her in instantly.

But cats have evolved as highly skilled solitary hunters. They have no pack or family to support an ailing member in the wild. They have developed the habit of hiding any sign of weakness and pain, rather than risk another predator spotting they are weak and turning hunter into prey. It is their natural instinct to disguise any symptoms of illness until it is extreme.

Instead of relying on Pandora herself to show she needs me, I have had to train Pandora's owner to check those claws herself regularly every time she has her own manicure done. We have also arranged for Pandora to see one of our qualified nurses for a feline mani/pedi at least every six weeks, as I cannot bear the thought of her having to go through that kind of totally preventable pain ever again.

In the same way, you need to watch over your furry friend, and know what is normal for her, so that you can react quickly to any subtle changes or issues.

Key Points:

- **Learn what is normal for your pet, both in their behaviour and when you check them over.**
- **Develop a routine of checking their eyes, ears, teeth, claws, skin and coat every day.**
- **Do not assume that just because they are not complaining there is nothing wrong.**

CHAPTER 5
PEAK CONDITION

Prevention is the best cure – keeping on top of your pet's routine appointments is the best way to maintain their health

Cats are perhaps one of the simplest pets to keep. They like to be clean, go to the toilet outside and (with any luck) rarely need veterinary attention. But there are some small things that are worth thinking about as your new cat settles in.

To keep your cat in peak condition, your pet requires a health check at least every six months. For pets over seven years old, this health check should include at least a urine sample, blood pressure check and thorough physical examination by your vet. You can read more about our Life Begins at 7 programme in Chapter 8.

We always complete a cat's Life Begins at 7 health check by recommending the very best food for their current health and situation. After all, the motto 'you are what you eat' applies just as much to cats as to humans!

At The Mewes Vets we always weigh your pet and record their weight every time we see them, regardless of whether they are poorly or just having a routine check-up. Many cats show weight changes throughout the year, becoming more active and fit in the summer, and getting less exercise if it's a bad winter. We then find these charts of their weight over time incredibly useful if a subtle problem crops up, or an owner is worrying about how much a pet is eating. The scales never lie!

Vaccinations

A vaccine is generally injected once a year to avoid the risk of potentially fatal infections. This also allows your pet to visit a cattery, if you would ever like to go away for more than one night – most catteries will not accept your pet unless they have been vaccinated.

The minimum requirement for cattery boarding is for your cat to be protected against cat flu. This has to be updated every 12 months, by a simple injection under the skin that most cats in my hands barely notice. Cat flu is highly contagious, just as human flu is, and cattery owners need to protect their reputations by avoiding an outbreak.

This vaccine is combined with a shot against panleucopenia, which I am pleased to say is rarely seen in areas where pets are regularly vaccinated. This disease has virtually died out thanks to the vaccine.

But we recommend more than just the base essentials for our pet cats who are allowed outdoors. These little ones are at risk of the highly fatal feline leukaemia, which gradually kills over several years, allowing plenty of time for sufferers to potentially spread the virus around. There is no treatment for feline leukaemia, so we strongly encourage vaccination as the only way to protect your furry friend from a slow but certain death.

To learn more about why vets recommend regular vaccination for cats, go to www.vaccinationsforyourcat.co.uk.

Neutering

Most pets are neutered by the time they reach middle age, but if yours is not, I recommend you make arrangements to have this done for their future wellbeing. Females who have litters as often as their systems allow not only cause our rescue societies to be overfull of cats needing homes, but also usually die young.

Male adult cats can be unattractive companions as they have a distinctive smell, often get into fights - which can be expensive when their injuries need resolving - and may prefer to be out of the home a great deal, so are not great companions. And of course, it is these individuals that father the litters that fill our rescue charities!

Parasite control

Whether your pet goes outside or not, all cats need regular parasite control. We can advise on a personal programme suited to your pet's expected lifestyle and habits. Those that hunt are more likely to be exposed to tapeworm, for instance, than couch potatoes!

Whilst planning your pet's personalised parasite programme, we will discuss the risks of having a flea infestation in your home, and how to get rid of them and prevent them returning. We will help you teach your children good hygiene around pets, and advise on a wormer that prevents the risk of nasty roundworms that can even cause a child to lose their sight.

The cat roundworm is called Toxocara cati. It has a very clever survival mechanism. Not only do its eggs last for several years in the environment, but it can also infect a variety of host species including foxes, rats and mice. Once inside a cat some of the worms form cysts and become dormant. These are then re-activated if the cat is a queen and becomes pregnant.

The worms mature as the pregnancy proceeds, and are eventually passed via the milk into the newborn kittens. So nearly all kittens are born infected with Toxocara. Even if treated in kittenhood, some Toxocara hide in new cysts in this next generation's muscles, where a wormer cannot kill them. These cysts re-activate at intervals, re-infesting the kitten as it grows and throughout its life, even if they never go outside.

When a person is infected by a roundworm, it wanders all round their body. This can result in a variety of issues including blindness, lung problems and allergic complaints including rheumatoid arthritis. Therefore we recommend routine treatment of kittens and cats at regular intervals throughout their lives, not only to protect their health but yours too!

Julia's Mewesings:

How to give a cat a pill...

You have probably heard the joke that goes round about how to give your cat a pill. It includes retrieving the cat from under your bed and down from the ceiling, and ends with you in A&E. But it is not so funny when your vet says you really must get a course of pills down your kitty's throat.

Nowadays we are fortunate to have many alternatives to giving medication by mouth, but there are still situations where I have no choice but to prescribe tablets.

If it is a single dose I will administer it myself, but the problems can start when a course is needed. Then I use my judgement to assess the situation, in a kind of risk-benefit ratio. I weigh up the risk that the cat's owner might get injured or that their pet will lose faith in them, against the benefit to the little one's long term health. This depends a great deal on the pet's attitude (or as I often call it - 'cattitude'). There are some cats that even I cannot give a pill to!

The most obvious choice, if your cat is not off its food, is to crush the pill and mash it into a soft special treat. Cats can be especially fond of tinned tuna, salmon paste, or even cream cheese. For others a small saucer of warmed milk can conveniently conceal some medication. You probably know what favourite treat your own pet prefers.

If your cat is too clever to fall for that trick, but is calm and gentle, then you can learn to open their mouth and pop the tablet to the back of their throat. We have an excellent video about how this is done on our website at www.themewesvets.co.uk/the-urban-vet. The main detail is to think in terms of getting the pill down their throat, not putting it on their tongue, as this will easily be spat out by a reluctant patient.

However, for many cats, the best bet is to find an alternative means of getting a dose in. These options can include long acting injections, diets that can suit certain illnesses, and the spot-on wormer, which is a liquid applied onto the skin. Much easier than risking a run-in with your cat's fangs!

Insurance

It is worth taking out an insurance policy to cover unexpected vets' fees, if your cat is not already beyond the age for cover. If they are, consider putting aside a little every month for a rainy day. Treatment of thyroid disease, for example, can top £4,000, and a broken leg can easily cost £3,000. Some things are not covered by pet insurance, particularly dental problems, so a rainy day fund is useful even for insured cats.

Julia's Mewesings:

Pretty Mollie - a 12 year old short haired cat - needed some teeth out. This was estimated at a cost of around £350, which her owner simply did not have. Luckily the dental treatment was paid for with her prize money when she won a phone-in competition - 'Name the Intro' - on a local commercial radio station, but one cannot hope to always be so lucky.

Similarly, poor Beanz was a young cat who suffered a fractured pelvis and dislocated hip. His caring owner was devastated when she realised that she had failed to make adequate provision for this type of emergency, and how much the cost of putting him right was going to be.

Ignoring the problem was not an option. He needed an operation called an excision arthroplasty to avoid constant pain. Luckily Beanz' owner was about to celebrate her birthday. Her Mum arranged for all her friends to bring cash instead of presents to her party, and this just covered the unexpected cost.

Keep an eye on household substances and decorations that could pose a problem to your cat...

If this is the first time you have welcomed a cat into your home, you need to have a little look around. For instance, flowers such as lilies are gorgeous, but they are poisonous to cats. If you have children you probably never leave medicines lying around, but if not, remember that the same precautionary rules apply to pet cats! I have known cats to steal all kinds of medicines designed for people, many of which were potentially fatal to their little feline bodies.

Other hazards include chewing gum and especially nicotine replacement gum, which contains a toxic substance called xylitol. If you have dogs, be especially careful to check every time you plan to apply a spot-on, especially if you bought it from somewhere other than a veterinary surgery. There are some out there that are extremely toxic to a cat; never put a dog spot-on onto your cat!

In the garden, make sure you only use pet safe slug pellets, and be super careful where you store the battery fluid drained out of your car battery. This stuff is incredibly toxic but very attractive to cats, who will go back and poison themselves a second time, if I manage to save their lives after the first incident!

To read more about potential hazards to your new best friend, go to: www.toxicdangerstoyourcat.co.uk.

Key Points from this chapter:

- Your cat needs an annual vaccination, as well as health checks every six months.
- Ensure your pet is neutered.
- Ask your vet for a personalised parasite program that will protect your pet as well as your family.
- Insure your pet, or save for a rainy day. None of us stay healthy forever - there will be vet's bills!
- Do a risk assessment of your home and garden, looking for things that may harm your new friend.

CHAPTER 6
ORGANISED FOR HOLIDAY

Going on holiday? If you're leaving your cat at home while you travel, make sure you've chosen their carer wisely

When it comes to booking holidays, I hope you are not like me - a 'last minute Minnie'? I find it incredibly hard to make a decision. I can often end up leaving it too late. And when I do finally set it all up there is that sudden jolt - who will look after my beloved dog Jazzy?

I really should get more organised. There are now plenty of options, and we do keep a list of them at Reception at the Clinic!

For cat owners, the traditional route of catteries is an obvious one, but you do need to book well ahead, as especially good facilities always get booked up in advance. The one you choose should remind you at the point of booking about the importance of your pet's vaccines being up-to-date.

If they don't, then you can assume they are not insisting on it with other pets, which means that your best friend's health could be at risk. If this is the case, book them in somewhere else.

The best way to choose a cattery for your beloved pet is to have visited several before making your choice - so do this now. Don't leave it till the last minute. Check how relaxed the current visitors seem, and look around at the cleanliness of the facilities. Does it smell? Are the food bowls caked up with dried-on food?

You will quickly form an opinion about the people and the facilities that your pet might be in, and decide if it is suitable for use or not.

There is also more interest in pet sitters, as opposed to catteries, around Sussex. You should check before booking that they are fully insured, have good references as cat lovers, and how much they are going to charge for their service.

The very best arrangement, of course, would seem to be when a family member or neighbour pops in to feed your cat twice a day. The only problem with that is that they may not see your pet, who could be outside having fun, or curled up under the shed with a broken leg.

This arrangement is probably perfect for cats who never go out, and possibly for those who always turn up at a specific feeding time. But it is a lot to ask of a friend to go hunting for a missing cat, and then to make the judgement that they are unwell, catch them and get them down to the vets.

Ideally your friend would commit to actually cuddling the cats and giving them a little love every time they pop in, just to get a feel for whether they are well and happy. This is a bigger favour than just dumping down some food, unless of course you can return the favour for their cats when they go away.

If you have booked your feline friend into a cattery whilst you are going away, then it is worth preparing for the journey a little ahead. Nothing is more likely to stress your new cat than you yourself trying to do things with them in a hurry. Make sure you pack their favourite food and toys well in advance, and a couple of blankets or pillows with a home scent on them. Give yourself plenty of time to get the little one into the travel box before your departure deadline. It's not as easy as you'd think!

It is quite common for an errant feline to miss a vet appointment with me. Tibby the cat failed to turn up for her regular check up. When I bumped into her owner a few days later she apologised and explained that the wily little beast had completely declined to be put into her travel basket.

As this happens fairly regularly, I reassured her that cats seem to have a sixth sense about avoiding veterinary appointments.

Here are my tips on how to persuade your feline friend into a basket:

First, make your own life easy. Choose a top opening basket, so that you have a nice wide area to pass them through. Alternatively the doorway should not have any kind of edging around it narrowing the opening, as this provides a perfect springboard for the puss to brace themselves on.

Next, try leaving the box lying around in the house with the door open and a favourite cushion inside. This allows your pet to be comfy around it, and maybe even choose it as a preferred place to sleep. For these cats you can just shut the door and go.

Then on the day of the appointment, keep your pet indoors for several hours beforehand - overnight if necessary - and shut the cat flap, doors and windows.

When it's time to get ready, start by moving your pet into a room with nothing they can crawl under, and shut them in. Do this before you locate the travel box and find an old bath towel. I find that the easiest way is to have the box on the floor, with its door wide open and at the top. So even if it is a side opener, turn it to stand the wrong way up so it becomes a top opener.

Then quietly place the towel over your cat, and immediately scoop them up and into the basket while still wrapped. The towel prevents them seeing what your plan is, and also prevents them using their claws effectively to resist the box. Then simply slip the door shut and fasten it. Leave them to work out how to unwrap themselves, it will take their minds off the fact that you won!

If your pet finds travelling a challenge, accompanying your journey with a loud chorus of protests, have a word with us about the product called Feliway©. This is a simple spritz applied into the cat box before travelling, which releases a pheromone designed to relax cats and help them feel more at home and less stressed on the journey.

Key Points from this chapter:

- **Have a plan for your new cat for when you would like to go on holiday.**

- **Visit some catteries now & remember to make a cattery booking as soon as you commit to the holiday.**

- **Make their travel box into a welcoming place for them to sleep.**

Chapters 7 to 12, which follow, describe some specific feline medical diseases

At my Clinic I have always made an effort to surround myself with people who are as passionate about pets as I am. Over the years we have developed a special proficiency in the care of older pets, so much so that you might say we are experts in geriatric care!

In the following chapters you will read about the six most common disorders that affect older cats, and learn more about how to spot them and what can be done to help. These include dental disease, thyroid disease, kidney problems, high blood pressure issues, joint problems and arthritis, and brain ageing or dementia. These can all be treated by teams like ourselves who are passionate about the care of older cats.

If you cannot find the relevant problem discussed here, I suggest you call my friendly experienced team on 01444 456886, or go to the Symptom Checker at www.themewesvets.co.uk

CHAPTER 7
THYROID DISEASE

A hungry cat that's still losing weight could have a thyroid problem

Julia's Mewesings:

"Arwen has a wonderful appetite. She keeps begging for more food. But it's a bit odd, she's been losing weight too…" As soon as I heard this, alarm bells began to ring in my head.

Arwen is a special friend who I have known for years. These symptoms sounded to me like I should be checking her thyroid gland.

One of the most common disorders that affects the geriatric cat, other than tooth problems, is a disease called hyperthyroidism.

This is caused by a (usually) tiny growth in the cat's thyroid gland, resulting in a dramatic over-production of the thyroid hormone. Humans can suffer from this too, and both experience similar but not identical symptoms.

In cats, they are typically desperately hungry, eating like they cannot stop, but still lose weight and become very thin. They can also suffer upset stomachs, their coats become moth-eaten, and they may seek out cool spots to sleep in rather than the warm and cosy spaces that cats normally occupy.

Hyperthyroidism is easy to diagnose with a blood test, assuming you have wonderful nurses like mine who can acquire a blood sample out of two and a half kilos of cranky old cat! The choice of subsequent treatment, however, does require some discussion. We soon were phoning Arwen's Mum with the confirmation of the diagnosis, and suggesting that she started treatment.

In Pharmacology, one of the great aims is to find or make a medication that very specifically targets only the abnormal diseased tissues, whilst sparing the healthy tissues of the patient. In other words, the theoretical drug would only kill cancer cells but not the stomach lining, for example, or target invasive viruses without harming the mammal they are attacking.

In thyroid medicine this concept has been well used. We can safely inject hyperthyroid patients with iodine that has been made radioactive. The radioactivity is of exceptionally short range - just millimetres - and short-lived. Only the cat's thyroid gland is affected, making it a supremely safe and gentle medication.

The treatment process is so amazingly elegant. The cat cannot feel a thing, and sits in a lead-lined hospital room whilst the radioactivity quietly and gently targets just its abnormal thyroid gland - the only part of the body where iodine is concentrated from the bloodstream. The pet is then cured for life, with no extra cost, no anaesthetic, and no unnecessary trauma.

There are other ways to treat hyperthyroidism in cats, including tablets for life, surgery under anaesthesia - which is usually repeated 2-3 years later - and dietary changes. My preferred option is the radioactive treatment because of its elegance, success rate, and minimal trauma to our sensitive little friends.

Key Points from this chapter:

- **If your middle-aged cat is showing an excellent appetite, but still losing weight, arrange to see your vet for a check-up.**
- **Hyperthyroidism is very common, but easy and inexpensive to treat.**

CHAPTER 8
KIDNEY DISEASE

Your older cat is more likely to suffer from particular conditions, including kidney disease. Make sure they have regular check-ups to keep them healthy and happy

Julia's Mewesings:

I didn't know Blackie at all, but I could tell straight away that she wasn't well.

My records indicated that her last visit was over 10 years ago, and her owner confirmed that she hadn't seen a vet in ages.

Her coat was out of condition, scruffy and dull. She was desperately thin, her bones visible along her spine, and her eyes were dull and sunken.

Her owner described some months of gradual worsening weight loss, and pickiness about her food, but what had finally caused him to bring her in was the constant vomiting, which had evolved about a week ago.

I didn't like the look of things, and as I gently moved her onto the scales I noted she was showing signs of dehydration, and had lost over 50% of the weight we had recorded when she was in her prime.

After a careful physical exam, which confirmed that she had several rotten teeth in her mouth, and swollen kidneys, I looked for a gentle way to break the news that there might be little I could do. Her owners were devastated, but philosophical. A blood test and urine sample confirmed my suspicion that she was already in the advanced stages of severe kidney disease.

I did not share with them that if she had been brought to me when the weight loss started I might have been able to make a huge difference to the outcome. Instead I started preparing them for a hard decision.

Blackie was one of several cats who created a real sense of frustration for me. Their owners were making false assumptions about their health and what vets could do to help them.

I was regularly seeing individuals who had not had check-ups for four or five years, and then they would arrive on my table, two-thirds of the weight they were last time, usually vomiting, off their food, drinking lots and generally feeling pretty awful.

What they all had in common was advanced kidney disease.

I talked it over with my team at The Mewes Vets and we began a crusade that became known as the Life Begins @ 7 Club.

With the Life Begins @ 7 Club, we encourage all owners of apparently healthy cats to bring their pets in for a thorough health check and examination – even if they seem fine - every six months. We know that kidney disease can be detected on a simple urine test well before any symptoms (like weight loss or anorexia) appear for an owner to notice.

One of the joys of the programme has been putting off the medical crisis that is advanced kidney disease by detecting, medicating and supporting cats with the earliest signs of a problem. Research has shown that cats whose vets have a programme like this for spotting renal disease early, and whose owners initiate appropriate support, live two to three years longer than those who don't.

We encourage the owners of every cat who is seven years old or over to pop into the Clinic every six months for their older well-pet check. Your cat will be weighed, and this weight will be monitored over time. We will help you collect a urine sample, as well as examining your pet: providing a dental check, a thyroid check, a heart and lung auscultation, and carefully looking for any unusual lumps and bumps. We may also advise a blood test.

Once we have a full picture of your pet's health we will hopefully celebrate with you about how well they are, or, if issues have been identified, we will talk to you about how we can help.

For more information on the Life Begins @ 7 Club, simply call our expert team on 01444 456886, or visit www.themewesvets.co.uk. You can also download more information at www.youroldercat.co.uk.

Key Points from this chapter:

- **Kidney problems are very common in older cats. This is a condition best spotted early, before medical symptoms are apparent.**

- **Ensure your pet is signed up on a regular screening programme with your vet.**

- **When diagnosed in the early stages, your vet can prescribe support which will dramatically and inexpensively improve improve your cat's long term good health.**

CHAPTER 9
YOUR CAT'S SIGHT

Don't risk your pet becoming permanently blind
– if they have a problem with their vision, take them to a
vet straight away

Julia's Mewesings:

"Quick! We need to see the Vet straight away! Socks has gone blind!" This is not a phrase you want to hear, but Socks' owner was told to bring him straight to me.

In that same month I had had two cats seek my help for the same problem. The first one, an attractive tortoiseshell called Lily, had seemed perfectly normal when her family retired for the night.

They came down the next morning and noticed that Lily seemed to have lost her sight. Assuming nothing could be done for her, they left it, finally deciding to seek my assistance a week later.

But later the same month, we got the call about Socks and rushed him straight into the Clinic. He was a cranky black and white soul, for whom co-operation was tricky. He had been losing a bit of weight, and perhaps was drinking a little more, but what had brought his owners rushing in that day was that he had suddenly started bumping into things around the home that morning.

In both Lily and Socks' cases I was able to recognise that the cats had experienced detachment of the retinas - the light sensitive inner linings of their eyeballs. I took their blood pressures, and a blood sample from them both. They were both suffering from the early signs of kidney disease, which are quite manageable, but the problems with the kidneys had caused their blood pressures to become abnormally high. This hypertension in their bloodstreams had resulted in their retinas effectively just blowing off.

As Socks' problem was very recent I was able to confidently predict a return of his sight within days by prescribing tablets to bring down his blood pressure. He learnt to accept these tablets (somewhat against his principles!) and began to receive supportive care for his kidneys. He went on to live for many comfortable, sighted years.

Lily was not so lucky. After seven days of floating free from their moorings her retinas were no longer able to re-attach themselves where they belonged. Her sight was totally – and permanently - lost. Her family and I were forced to reluctantly make the decision to let her go, as she was not adapting at all well to her new disability and seemed distressed.

Julia's Mewesings - continued:

Pets that gradually lose their sight over months often adapt to their new circumstances, but this had been too sudden.

So now I have many conversations with owners of older cats, coaching them that if ever their little pet seems to have suddenly lost their sight they are to bring them to me the same day, as miracles are definitely possible.

High blood pressure, or hypertension, is apparently very common in humans, for many reasons, some of which do not apply to cats.

In fact, you might think that cats are the most relaxed and lazy creatures, so probably would be much less prone to blood pressure issues than us worrying humans with our stress-filled lives and high fat diets.

The reality is that some cats are the epitome of cool, whilst others live their lives in a state of constant anxiety, just like us. But this is not what usually causes them to suffer high blood pressure - it's kidney disease, and occasionally hyperthyroidism. You can read more about these in Chapters 7 and 8.

At first, when the blood pressure in the cat's circulation becomes too high you may see some bleeding into the eyeball, but this is easily missed unless very severe. Often the first time cat owners realise there is an eye problem is only when the cat is completely blind.

High blood pressure can also cause issues such as bleeding into the brain, with resultant abnormalities including fitting and dementia; it damages the heart by making it work harder than it otherwise might; and also damages the kidneys, creating a vicious circle of problems.

There is no way to spot hypertension in a human or a cat without taking the trouble to measure it.

Failing to measure and record a patient's blood pressure regularly risks missing an opportunity to easily and inexpensively correct a potentially very serious or even fatal situation.

At The Mewes Vets we encourage every owner of a cat over seven years of age to allow us to inexpensively measure and record their blood pressure at least every six months.

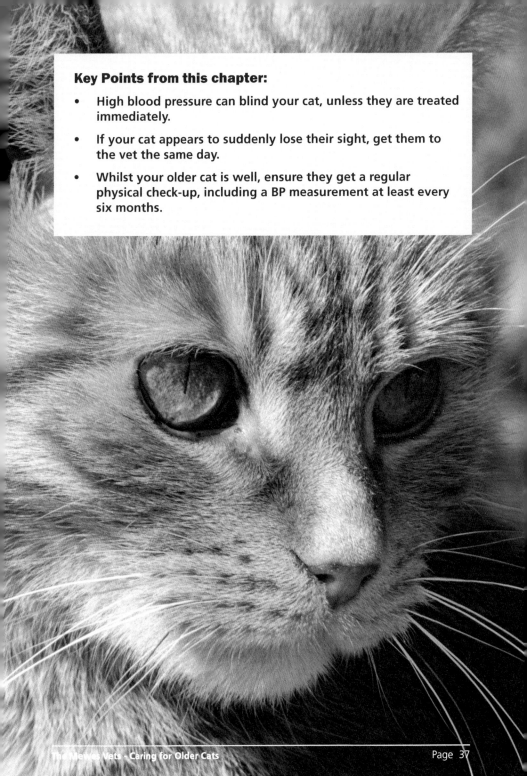

Key Points from this chapter:

- High blood pressure can blind your cat, unless they are treated immediately.

- If your cat appears to suddenly lose their sight, get them to the vet the same day.

- Whilst your older cat is well, ensure they get a regular physical check-up, including a BP measurement at least every six months.

CHAPTER 10
DENTAL ISSUES

Don't let your cat be part of the 85% who suffer from unnecessary dental disease at some point in their life

As a vet, one of my biggest problems can be persuading owners of cats that their pet's teeth really do need intervention. If only cats imitated small children and gripped their cheeks whilst yowling, my job would be a whole lot easier!

But I know it's all worthwhile when cat owners come back in and thank me for making their pet's lives so much better by extracting rotten teeth, which is just what happened with Jess.

Julia's Mewesings:

At Jess' routine vaccination I recognised holes in the enamel of several of her teeth; this was painfully exposing her pulp. Her owner's response was typical: "Are you sure she needs teeth out? She's been eating fine."

Fortunately, my explanation that Jess was simply hiding her discomfort, as befits a lone huntress, satisfied her owner, who allowed me to keep Jess for a day and extract the four damaged teeth under full general anaesthetic.

When I saw her one week later, her sockets were already healing brilliantly and her owner was amazed at the change in her playfulness and attitude.

"It's like you've taken years off her!" she said. She was really pleased that she had trusted me and let me help Jess.

This happens so often that I have started asking owners to give me testimonials so that other anxious cat owners can be reassured.

It is thought that as many as 85% of cats aged three years and older have dental disease of one sort or another.

There are two main reasons why things go wrong in a cat's mouth with time. One is that, unlike us people, they do not brush their teeth every day. The other is the condition that Jess suffered from, which only cats get, called Feline Resorptive Lesions (FRLs).

A cat's mouth is full of germs at all times, and these build up into a multi-storey car park of germs on the teeth. At first this is soft and could brush away, or be eliminated by a good quality dental biscuit. At this stage is it called plaque.

With time this hardens into tartar, which only an ultrasonic scaler machine can break off the surface of the crowns, which in pets requires a general anaesthetic to use.

A build-up of germs on the teeth can contribute to gum disease or gingivitis, and mouth issues like stomatitis.

FRLs are seen in all cats, even lions, but in no other species. We still are not sure why they appear, but it is as if the enamel on the crown has just disappeared leaving a hole, which the gum tries to fill or grow over, leaving a discreet area of swelling and inflammation over the base of a tooth. Unfortunately, the only known treatment is extraction of the painfully damaged tooth.

To read more about the symptoms of tooth problems in cats, visit www.felinedentaldisease.co.uk to download a free guide.

Key Points from this chapter:

- Cats are really good at concealing pain, especially toothache. You will probably not know if they have a bad tooth.

- Most cats need a tooth or two extracted as they get older. Be prepared for this cost, so that you can keep their mouths healthy and comfy.

- Most dental problems are not covered by pet insurance.

CHAPTER 11
ARTHRITIS

Just like humans, cats can also develop arthritis in old age. Help your pet to stay comfortable and pain-free as long as possible

Julia's Mewesings:

Jenson was not pleased to see me. Known as a feisty character at the Clinic, he was already giving me the eye when I opened up his travel box.

"He has been hopping on his hind leg occasionally," his owner shared. I chatted with her about his symptoms whilst allowing him to adapt to his arrival, and then respectfully encouraged him out onto my exam table to perform a mobility examination.

I now do this for every pet over seven years old, at their regular six month check-ups. A recent veterinary lecture I attended confirmed the understanding within the profession that cats are really bad at letting us know when they are in pain. The consensus is that they may become less active as a result of pain, but many owners accept this decline in activity as 'just old age creeping in'.

However, our finding is that cats can experience quite severe discomfort and successfully conceal it. Jenson was a good example.

With a sympathetic nurse's assistance, I manipulated Jenson's left back leg and was quickly able to establish an obvious reason for the problem. He had dislocated his knee cap. It kept slipping in and out of position under my fingers, and all the associated ligaments that normally kept it in position were torn or abnormally stretched.

I know from a colleague who suffered the same injury that this is screamingly painful. Yet Jenson just gave me a slightly pained look, not dissimilar to his usual supercilious expression.

His owner and I agreed on a non-surgical solution to his problem, and six months later his knee cap had settled down and he was walking normally on all four paws again. However, arthritis was an inevitable outcome after such an injury to this important joint.

Jenson is an example of a pet who is now part of my 'pyramid of care' for arthritis. The foundations of my pyramid are:

- To manage the individual's weight so that the joints are not under unnecessary pressure;

- To optimise exercise so that joints and muscles are loosened up regularly;

- To use natural products & non surgical therapies that aid joint healing such as acupuncture, hydrotherapy and physiotherapy where appropriate;

- To provide anti-inflammatories and then painkillers.

I recognise in a large proportion of my feline friends that they are experiencing reduced movement and pain in their joints, necks and backs, usually without ever complaining, unlike Jenson who at least gave us a clue. But they still have the right to a comfortable old age, so I will continue to do my very best to educate their owners and help their pets experience a long and pain-free retirement.

If your older pet has not had a mobility check recently, call my friendly team on 01444 456886 and arrange an appointment.

To read more about helping cats with stiffness, limping or other issues with their mobility go to www.keepingmycatmoving.co.uk

Key Points from this chapter:

- Cats are very good at hiding their pain, so make sure you get them checked over regularly for any problems or injuries!

- Do not put a change in exercise patterns down to just old age. It may be arthritis and be treatable.

Image from taymtaym, https://www.flickr.com/photos/taymtaym

CHAPTER 12

DEMENTIA

Elephants might be immune to forgetfulness, but dementia can be a serious problem for older cats

Julia's Mewesings:

Splodge has been under my care for years, and is a character I feel I know well. She has a loving owner, and has never been too much of a worry to her. But at a recent Life Begins @ 7 check up a new problem cropped up.

"It's like she's become nocturnal," her owner complained. "She's waking us up at night, but she doesn't seem to want anything. It's driving us mad!"

It struck me that Splodge might be suffering from feline dementia, which is relatively newly recognised. Her owner and I elected to perform some thorough checks to ensure that she was not suffering from any other complicating conditions, before attempting to support her brain function.

Splodge had her urine checked, blood test taken and her blood pressure measured. I also performed a really thorough clinical examination, and was able to confirm that several teeth needed extraction. Her other tests indicated it should be safe to anaesthetise her, so I dealt with her oral problems.

However her owner still reported being disturbed every night, and she herself was starting to look a little haggard.

So we introduced some simple changes into Splodge's life, including an optimal diet to prevent further deterioration of her teeth and to support the cognitive function of her brain. Her owner started playing simple games with her in the daytime to keep her more mentally active, and we trialled some therapy for dementia.

Things have improved dramatically now for Splodge's owner, who is getting some sleep again, and we feel that Splodge herself has a much improved quality of life.

We all love our feline friends, but what happens when their brains start to deteriorate? Nowadays there is much more we can do to help them than in previous times.

Recent surveys have found that around 30% of cats over seven years old show behavioural changes, and this increases to 50% in cats over 15 years old.

What causes it?

There are many causes of the symptoms of dementia, from arthritis to high blood pressure (hypertension), or kidney, thyroid, liver, intestinal or even dental disease. I usually start investigating by giving the pet a thorough examination, and then some tests such as urine and blood analysis and a blood pressure measurement.

If the owner and I agree that all other causes have been ruled out or managed, then a diagnosis of Cognitive Dysfunction Syndrome (CDS) may be made. Of course, many older cats have more than one problem, so I sometimes recommend sorting out bad teeth, looking after some kidney issues and dealing with arthritis, for example, as well as tackling the CDS.

CDS itself is thought to be caused by a problem with the blood supply to the brain, and by long term free radical damage to brain cells.

Our nurses will discuss a diet rich in nutrients that will help by reducing further free radical damage to the brain. In studies cats have lived longer, with enhanced brain function, become less sedentary, and showed less stress on optimal diets for CDS.

Environmental enrichment - including providing toys, more cuddles or companionship and interaction, and food hunting games - really helps too.

You should aim to maintain a routine of regular feeding times and other activities such as grooming and the locking of the cat flap. Avoid moving furniture around in the home, especially the litter tray, food and water bowls.

If your cat seems anxious, you can help them by using a Feliway© plug-in or Zylkene© - both natural calming substances.

There are also medications that may be appropriate for your pet. Your vet will make a recommendation, depending on the results of any medical tests performed.

If your cat has recently:

- been forgetting where things are, for example the litter tray, and so having accidents indoors;

- been crying loudly, especially at night;

- been showing increased attention seeking, aggression, anxiety, less tolerance of other pets in the household, or has been less responsive;

- shown changes in sleeping patterns;

- shown increased or decreased activity;

- been grooming themselves less than they used to;

- been increasingly forgetful - for example, forgetting they have just been fed...

...they may be showing signs of senility or Cognitive Dysfunction Syndrome and need our help.

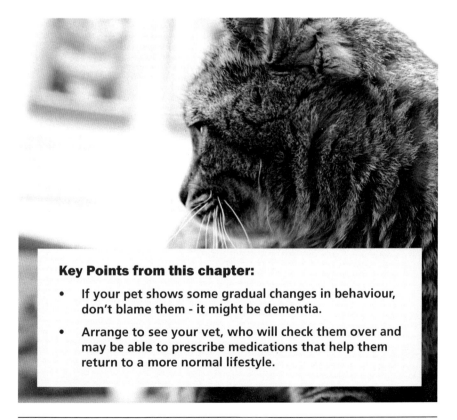

Key Points from this chapter:

- **If your pet shows some gradual changes in behaviour, don't blame them - it might be dementia.**

- **Arrange to see your vet, who will check them over and may be able to prescribe medications that help them return to a more normal lifestyle.**

CHAPTER 13
CHOOSE THE BEST VET

You wouldn't let just anyone look after your child's healthcare, would you? Your pet's health is important too, so it's essential to know what you're looking for in your new vet

Whether you have just got a new pet for the first time, or have been a pet owner for years, choosing a veterinary professional to care for your furry companion is an understandably important task.

Take the time to research your local vet practices properly – give them a call for a chat or to ask some questions about their practice, or even pop in to visit them if you can. You will soon get a feel for the ones who are warm, compassionate, and with knowledgeable and understanding staff who are genuinely interested in your pet.

Check out their websites too. Some practices offer short bios about their team, so you can see the sort of experience and interests they have, as well as getting a bit more of a feel for the individuals who'll be responsible for looking after your pet's health.

Whilst a flashy, futuristic, techy practice doesn't necessarily equate to top quality veterinary care, it is important that your chosen vet at least takes an interest in remaining up-to-date with advances in the veterinary field. This will make sure that they're always fully informed about possible symptoms and conditions, as well as new treatment options that might help your pet.

If you adopted your cat in their later years, speak to potential vet surgeries about their experience and provision for older animals. Some more advanced practices offer specific health plans or 'clubs' for older pets, so that they receive the specialist check-ups and necessary testing for conditions that are more likely to develop as they age.

As with humans, your pet's metabolism will also adjust with age, which makes them more susceptible to some sneaky weight gain! A good vet will either have a specific weight and diet clinic available to you, or will make use of nutritional advisors to offer help and support about your pet's food intake and lifestyle. Your pet's nutritional requirements will change as they get older, and it's important to keep up with these adjustments to ensure that they remain in great health for as long as possible.

Finally, it is crucial that you trust your vet to act in your pet's best interests. The very best practices will guarantee to always see your pet as soon as they can if you are worried about them, rather than placating you with generic phone advice and persuading you to "come back if the problem continues". You should never feel like you're inconveniencing your vet, but rather that they are always happy to see you and your pet, and take the time to give a proper examination and consultation at every visit. A good vet will listen to your concerns, view your pet as an individual and make a recommendation based on the best course of action for them – regardless of price – whilst making sure you are always aware of your options.

If you need any further advice about anything that I have covered in this book, or to experience an exemplary veterinary practice first-hand (you didn't think I would get to the end of this chapter without a shameless plug, did you?), just give **The Mewes Vets a call on 01444 456886.**

I hope you've enjoyed this short guide, perhaps even learned a few things, and are looking forward to spending many happy years with your new cat!

Key Points from this chapter:

- If possible, visit any prospective vet surgeries before you choose the one to care for your cat – get a feel for them, talk to their team and see whether you feel like you would trust them to look after your little companion.

- Your chosen vet should treat your pet as an individual, recommending a tailored course of action where possible rather than treating them as a generic case.

- It's important that your vet has the appropriate facilities and knowledge in place to care for your cat as they age – including check-ups, vaccinations, and diet & weight management advice.

I would like to thank these kind friends for allowing me to use their photographs: Pauline Fowler, Andrew Lloyd, Woody Salvage, Denise Scutt.